# A–Z

## OF

# BRISTOL

PLACES - PEOPLE - HISTORY

Cynthia Stiles

AMBERLEY

# Acknowledgements

I would like to thank my husband David and daughter Sharon for their invaluable help in producing this book. All modern photographs by Cynthia and Sharon Stiles unless otherwise indicated.

First published 2019

Amberley Publishing
The Hill, Stroud, Gloucestershire, GL5 4EP
www.amberley-books.com

Copyright © Cynthia Stiles, 2019

The right of Cynthia Stiles to be identified as the Author of this work has been asserted in accordance with the Copyrights, Designs and Patents Act 1988.

ISBN  978 1 4456 8171 9 (print)
ISBN  978 1 4456 8172 6 (ebook)

British Library Cataloguing in Publication Data. A catalogue record for this book is available from the British Library.

Typesetting by Aura Technology and Software Services, India. Printed in Great Britain.

# Contents

# Introduction

Bristol has been reinventing itself continuously, which has always brought new people and new ideas into a city with many old traditions. From its beginnings it was a port and those of many nationalities have made their home here, some for generations, some for just long enough to make their mark before moving on.

Even in the early twentieth century Bristol had been called 'a grand muddle' and now may seem a city that has lost much of its past, through enemy action, bad planning and indiscriminate demolition. Glancing around, you see a lot of modern buildings of concrete, steel and glass. But scratch the surface and layers of history are uncovered, while here and there that history still remains in view, if you know where to look.

This book will give some insight of where to look to find out about the history of Bristol and the people who have lived and worked here over the centuries.

# A

## Arcade

Georgian Bristol aspired very much to be as fashionable as London, so after the Burlington Arcade opened in the capital, allowing shopping in all kinds of weather, a consortium of Michael Wrayford, John W. Hall and James Paty decided that Bristol should have one as well. On the laying of the foundation stone in May 1824 the local newspaper commented on how Bristol architecture was looked down on by visitors but this new development would be ushering in a new era of excellence.

The Arcade entrance in Broadmead.

The proprietors employed James and Robert Foster as architects. They used cast-iron and glazing in their design to give light and airiness to the covered streets of two-storey shops, making it an elegant promenade from St James Barton to Broadmead. There were originally two Arcades, known as the Upper and the Lower. There were gated entrances, which were locked on Sundays, as these were privately owned walkways not public roads, and even had a beadle at one time to make sure order was maintained.

The mix of shops changed over the years. In 1875, for example, as well as the trunk makers and milliners, booksellers and jewellers there was a phrenologist and a pub called the Shepherd's Return. In March 1893 a fire that started in a shop after closing time caused damage to a portion of the Lower Arcade glass roof. The buildings were then described as dingy, dirty and begrimed and a couple of months later, as there was a new proprietor, the whole of the Arcades was renovated and redecorated.

The German bombing raids of 1940 were far more disastrous, completely destroying the Upper Arcade and leaving the Lower Arcade seriously damaged. For a long while it looked as though both would be swept away but public protests won the day and the Lower Arcade was restored and is still in use today.

Interior of the Arcade.

# Ashman, Herbert

The first mayor of Bristol was appointed in 1216 but it wasn't until 1899 that the title was upgraded to that of Lord Mayor, as changes due to the Boundaries Act meant that Bristol was now a municipality with a population of 320,000. Herbert Ashman was the first Lord Mayor of Bristol and also achieved the rare distinction of being knighted by Queen Victoria from her carriage while he knelt in Corn Street outside the old Council House. It was the last personal conferment by the Queen. Herbert Ashman had succeeded his father in the family company of leather merchants, which was situated in Broadmead. The name can still be seen carved into the pediment. The use of leather was far more widespread in those days than now. It wasn't just for boots and shoes and bags; all sorts of machinery used leather driving belts and hoses, which were manufactured by the company.

He was described as a man 'with a shrewd command of prudence and resource, a marked capacity for business and a well-balanced knowledge of human nature, a public speaker of distinction'.

Nos 1–5 Broadmead, formerly the premises of Herbert Ashman and Co. Ltd.

# Avon Gorge

The Avon Gorge has been described as a miniature ravine and for centuries has made a lasting impression on all who have seen it. In the Middle Ages there were myths and stories about the place including tales of two giants, Goram and Vincent, or Ghyston, who created it, brothers seeking to alter the course of the river, rivals for the love of a fair maiden possibly, or just testing their prowess against each other, but always with a tragic ending.

Though composed mainly of carboniferous limestone, the high cliffs also contain bands of iron ore and veins of quartz, nicknamed Bristol diamonds. At the Great Fault a bed of millstone grit was forced up when the rocks were folded millions of years ago. The rocks contain many fossils of corals, shellfish and other ancient marine life. The river cut through all of this at the end of the last Ice Age.

During the eighteenth and nineteenth centuries quarrying activity changed the face of the gorge. Some amendments were carried out for making the passage of river traffic easier but mostly the removal of rock was for purely commercial purposes, especially for building the increasing number of houses. The Great Quarry and Black Rock Quarry operated for many years, stone from the latter being used, among other things, for pitching and paving in the city.

St Vincent's Rocks with Observatory.

The Avon Gorge from the Sea Walls.

But by the 1840s complaints were made in the newspaper not only 'expressing sorrow and surprise that for trifling gain so much beautiful and almost unequalled scenery should be destroyed', but also about the incessant noise of the workmen's implements. Concerns were raised regarding the safety of the public and those travelling on the river as blasting was happening at any time, with very little notice, causing stones to be hurled into the air with great force, in some cases causing injury. It took years, but finally all quarrying in the gorge ceased.

Along the top of Black Rock a Mr Wallis had built a wall back in the 1740s, as a preventative measure against people accidentally plunging over into the gorge. This area became known as the Sea Walls and is a marvellous viewpoint along the river. Many of the cliffs are clothed in greenery. Some plants are common wild flowers, others are rare, and a few, such as the whitebeam tree sorbus bristolensis, grow wild only in the gorge.

# Balloons

The Bristol International Balloon Fiesta is now firmly established as one of the favourite events in the city's calendar. However, a hot air balloon took to the Bristol skies as long ago as 24 September 1810. It was piloted by James Sadler of Oxford, who had made several flights when he was younger, then worked as an engineer and chemist before becoming an aeronaut once more.

Such a novelty attracted large crowds to Stokes Croft, where the ascent was being made. Here they saw a colourful silk balloon of green and light purple with a gold central band bearing the name of the Chancellor of Oxford. Sadler took with him William Clayfield, a young chemist from Bristol, and a cat. As the balloon rose into the air, the two men waved painted banners. Carried away by the north-easterly wind, they passed over Leigh Down where they dropped the cat in a basket which had a parachute attached. The cat survived, rescued by a lime burner, and was subsequently taken into the possession of the local doctor.

The balloon passed over the coast into the middle of the Bristol Channel where they released ballast, so they rose again and were off Lynton in Devon when they realised they were descending once more. Everything they could jettison went overboard, including a greatcoat, but there was not enough gas left to allow them to reach shore, so they landed in the water 4 miles out. Fortunately they had been seen and after an hour they were rescued, although it took another two to deflate and pack up the balloon.

Fourteen years later George Graham made a flight from Bristol in his balloon, taking off from Avon Street in St Philips with Robert Saunders, a solicitor. Graham had taken the precaution of having the gondola beneath lined with cork so it was buoyant, but although the vagaries of the wind meant that he crossed and recrossed the Avon and then hung almost static over the Severn at Aust, he did not end up in the water. He landed safely in a quarry at Itchington Common in Gloucestershire, a couple of hours after ascending.

Don Cameron MBE set up his company to manufacture balloons in Bristol in 1971, a small enterprise at first but now operating from large premises in Bedminster. The company specialises in special shape balloons and have built around a thousand over the years, many of which have flown at the Bristol International Balloon Fiesta.

*Right*: Special shape balloon Rupert Bear was brought back in 2018 by popular demand.

*Below*: Balloon Fiesta Nightglow. (Naomi Knott)

The festival started very small at Ashton Court in the 1970s, with a handful of balloons and the spectators able to wander close to the inflating canopies at the take-off in the early morning and evening. Now the fiesta is spread over four days and around 130 balloons take part. There are mass ascents morning and evening, dependent on the weather, but the balloons ascend from an arena and there are trade stands, fairground rides and other entertainment. The Night Glows on Thursday and Saturday, with tethered balloons pulsing light to music, end with fireworks displays.

# Blitz

The Luftwaffe bombing raids of the Second World War changed the heart of Bristol forever. On Sunday 24 November 1940 incendiaries and high explosives rained from the bombers in the sky, pulverising whole streets of houses and shops, leaving factories and warehouses gutted and ancient churches as roofless shells. Another big raid followed on 2 December with more in early 1941, one of which lasted for ten hours and another for twelve hours on a freezing cold night when water from the firemen's hoses made roads become skating rinks and dripped into huge icicles.

The 'Good Friday raid' on the night of 11 April 1941 was a double attack, resulting in more serious destruction. Prime Minister Winston Churchill, on his way to confer degrees at Bristol University, of which he was then Chancellor, had to spend that night on a train in a siding just outside the city. When he went around the worst hit areas shortly after his arrival in the morning, people were still being dug out of the ruins. At the degree ceremony he noted that many of those in academic robes still had underneath 'the soaked and grimy uniforms of their night's toil'.

Walking through Castle Park, it is difficult to imagine that this was once a bustling shopping area with department stores and cinemas. The skeleton of St Peter's Church stands as a reminder of the past but the adjacent richly carved, wooden, seventeenth-century St Peter's Hospital went up in flames so fierce that it could not be saved. The galleried Dutch House nearby was so fire-damaged that what remained had to be pulled down. Narrow St Mary-le-Port Street, with its gabled shops, stood no chance against the blaze and little but the tower remained of the church after which it was named. Where large, modern, plate glass windows had displayed their wares lay heaps of shattered glass and twisted girders.

It was decided after the war that this area should not be restored as a shopping area, as it was unsuitable for the car access that would be required in this new age. Broadmead, down the hill, would become the shopping area of the future. For two decades the forlorn site languished, used as a car park for part of this time. A 1951 guidebook to the West Country refers to the 'fascinating shrubbery area of bomb ruination' when describing Bristol. Then it was announced it would become a park, the setting for a new museum and art gallery. Eventually, with costs rising, the museum and art gallery idea was dropped and just the park was completed.

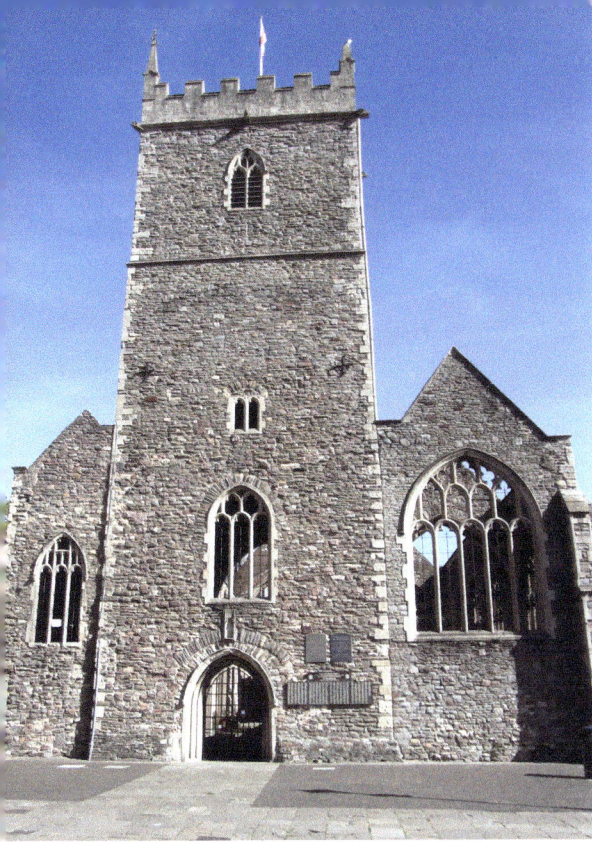

*Above left*: St Peter's, the oldest church in the city, destroyed by enemy action on 24 November 1940.

*Above right*: The tower of St Mary-le-Port Church.

*Below*: Castle Park, opened in May 1993, transformed from blitzed ruins.

The development of Broadmead as the new central shopping district was not popular with many store owners, as they wanted to rebuild where they had been before. In addition, several old buildings that had survived the Blitz were now demolished to accommodate the Broadmead area plan and the rather bleak concrete architectural style that had been decided on showed none of the variety that was there before. A lot of large square office blocks also made their appearance throughout central Bristol.

It wasn't just the very centre of Bristol that endured the many raids but that was the area that seemed most changed, almost obliterated, long-familiar landmarks gone. Amid the devastation there was much loss of life and serious injury. In 2008 plaques engraved with the names of the men, women and children who died in the greater Bristol area because of the Blitz were mounted on the front of St Peter's Church as a memorial.

# Bristol Bridge

The name Bristol comes from Brycgstow, the place of the bridge, though no one knows when exactly the first bridge was built or what it looked like. It was doubtless of wood and made a crossing of the River Avon possible without getting wet and muddy.

The old Bristol Bridge was lined with houses.

William Worcestre described the bridge that was there in the 1480s as 72 yards long and 5 yards wide with tall houses on either side, which projected over the water. It stood on massive stone piers, the water flowing through the arches. There was a public latrine on the Redcliffe side and stretching across the centre was the Chapel of St Mary with its square bell tower and a crypt that could apparently accommodate all the councillors and officers of the town for public meetings. The chapel itself had large stained-glass windows depicting the original benefactors who paid for the building, Elias Spelly and his family.

By the mid-1700s concern was growing about the state of the old bridge. It was now far too narrow for the amount of wheeled traffic it carried and those crossing on foot had to dodge and weave between, which led to serious accidents. An Act of Parliament was passed for the erection of a new bridge but to make a change would cause considerable disruption and expense, so decisions like where this new bridge should be sited were wrangled over and delayed. Getting a consensus on a design seemed near impossible, with some proposing a single arch and others arguing for multiple ones.

There were over seventy meetings held and it wasn't until November 1763 that a majority vote agreed it would be a bridge of three arches and it would be built

Bristol Bridge as it is today.

exactly where the old one was, to the design of the appropriately named architect, James Bridges. It was eventually opened in 1768. The commissioners had been given authority by the Act to collect tolls for using the bridge to the value of £32,000 to keep it in good repair and toll houses were positioned at each end. Once the costs had been covered, it was assured that these tolls would be abolished.

In September 1792 it was announced that the tolls would only be collected for one more year, so as that time in 1793 rolled round, people rushed across the bridge without paying while some hotheads pulled down the toll gates and the board showing the toll rates and burned them. The authorities at this moment declared that they still needed over £3,000 to defray the bridge costs anyway, so tolls would have to continue and new gates were installed. There was mayhem and Saturday night spectators gathered to watch as stacks of wood and rubbish were piled against the new gates and set alight.

The militia arrived and were pelted with stones by the crowd. Amid the hubbub, the magistrates read the Riot Act, to no avail. It took the militia firing over people's heads to disperse the crowd. Unfortunately it wasn't enough to quell the anger of the mob and the next day they gathered again, preventing tolls being collected and instigating another visit by soldiers. In the evening, when the soldiers left, more fires were set including to the toll house doors. A small military party was sent to put them out and, after doing so, once again retreated. The third time the militia marched up. Some were struck to the ground by items the crowd were throwing and there was a fusillade of angry shots from the soldiers, followed by more constant fire. Eleven people died from this action and many more were injured, but there was no official enquiry.

The toll houses remained in position but became shops. They were removed when the bridge was again widened in the late nineteenth century. James Bridges' bridge had been twice widened by 1900 and in the 1960s a steel parapet was added.

# Centre

St Augustine's Bridge was named so as it was over St Augustine's Reach near the end of Clare Street. The smaller ships still made their way to these quaysides and, to allow for this, the bridge was raised and lowered, so the more common

The Tramways Centre in the early 1900s.

name was the Drawbridge. The trouble was this manoeuvre took time and caused traffic hold-ups, sometimes of almost an hour, leading to increasing annoyance and complaints.

As early as 1837 people were demanding a wider fixed bridge, but this would mean the owners of quayside warehouses would no longer be able to unload their ships outside their premises. The arguments raged on for over half a century but at last agreement was reached to culvert the Frome, fill in the section above the bridge and build one that would allow passage of traffic at all times. The upper part of the infilled area was made into a broad tree-shaded avenue, but at the end nearest the bridge was a triangular piece of ground that was eagerly seized on by a prominent local entrepreneur.

George White was the managing director of the Bristol Tramways and Carriage Co., which had been running a large fleet of horse-drawn trams and buses around the city for several years, but White knew that electric trams were the way to go. He wanted a terminus for the vehicles, which would bring passengers from the suburbs to an easily defined point close to shops, offices and places of entertainment in the city. Acquiring this newly available site in 1895, he named it the Tramways Centre.

Trams displayed this name on their destination boards, and it was printed on tickets and timetables and advertising. It created some angry diatribes in the press about an area 'of public land' being acquired and peremptorily renamed by the BTCC. No one seems to have complained when it was later nicknamed Skivvies' Island because of the number of servants using the trams to get to work. In the end it just became known by Bristolians as the Centre.

# Christmas Steps

Christmas Steps is a steep little alley that was 'steppered done' in 1669 by Alderman Jonathan Blackwell, changing its appearance into a picturesque Bristol scene with a romantic-sounding name. Originally called Queen Street, it was known as that well into Victorian times. The lower end was by Christmas Street, which itself had started out as Knifesmiths' Street, the word mangled over the years.

Past the ancient gateway of St Bartholomew's Hospital, on the right-hand side going up, are old houses that became small shops. On the left is the back wall of the Fosters' Almshouses building that had shops built into the basement when it was rebuilt in the 1880s. The figures in niches in the wall, at around the centre of Christmas Steps, are from the Merchant Venturers' Hall in Marsh Street, which was one of the buildings destroyed in the Blitz. At the top are sedilia, stone seats which may have come from St Bartholomew's or the Chapel of the Three Kings of Cologne at the top, both of them being in existence since the Middle Ages.

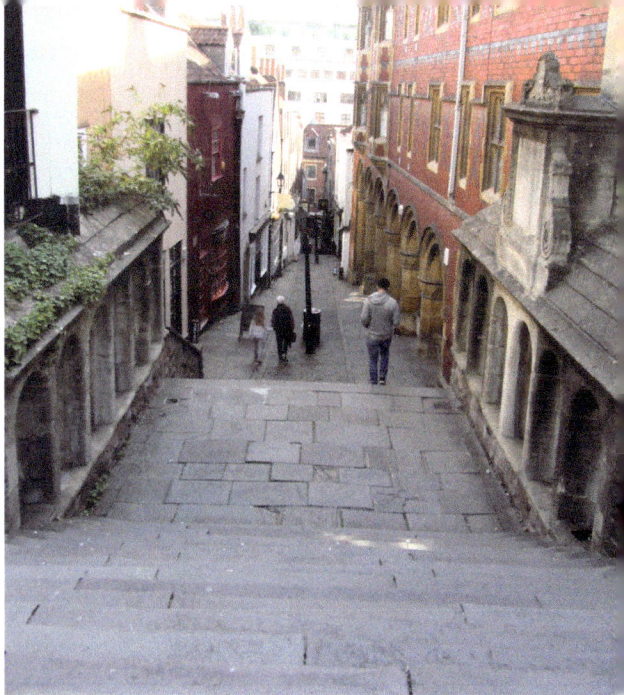

*Above left*: Christmas Steps viewed from the bottom.

*Above right*: Christmas Steps viewed from the top.

# Clifton Rocks Railway

There's plenty to see in Clifton, the village that grew up to become a prosperous Georgian suburb, and for forty years one way to get there was by using the Rocks Railway, which travelled in a vertical tunnel up St Vincent's Rocks from Hotwell Road to Sion Hill. The lower entrance was a castellated building, ornately lettered, while the upper entrance was a more discreet arched structure.

Some 100,000 passengers travelled on the Railway in the first six weeks of opening and it remained popular for the next few years, especially on weekends and holidays, but gradually the number of people using it on a regular daily basis diminished. It finally closed in 1934. During the Second World War the tunnels were adapted and used by the BBC. Studios and a technical control room were built inside and radio transmitters installed. The transmitter continued in use as a local booster station until 1960, when it became redundant. For years the railway lay disused and gradually mouldering away with damp.

The Clifton Rocks Railway Trust has been formed by a group of volunteers to restore the railway. The work is ongoing and has included clearing out much rubbish that had accumulated in the tunnel and the stations. Some of the original turnstiles, railings and light fittings that were found have been repaired and replaced on the site, gradually building up a picture of this remarkable abandoned piece of Bristol history.

Clifton Rocks Railway terminus on the Portway.

# College Green

The College part of the name comes from the fact that the cathedral, to which it belongs, was the collegiate church of the Abbey of St Augustine. It was originally known as the Sanctuary and the Abbey sheep were grazed here. When Henry VII visited Bristol in 1480, he and his retinue made a great procession around it.

It presented a very different appearance in the nineteenth century. It was enclosed by a wall with railings on top and access was by climbing a flight of steps from the pavement below. There were two rows of tall trees around the perimeter and avenues bordering the paths that crossed it.

It was flattened again between 1950 and 1954 when the new Council House (now known as City Hall) was built, so it could better complement the design, a less than popular move at the time. The starkness has softened over the years since then, with the growth of trees and some flower displays.

College Green in the early twentieth century.

A view of modern College Green.

# Dirac, Paul

The name Dirac may not be familiar to you but he was a mathematical and scientific giant. Born in Bristol in 1902 to a Swiss school teacher father and an English librarian mother, Paul Adrien Maurice Dirac became one of the foremost mathematicians and quantum scientists of the twentieth century.

He became notable in the field of quantum mechanics after studying and researching quantum theory and general relativity at Cambridge. Aged just twenty-two, Dirac had mastered quantum theory as it was then understood but disagreed with some of the ideas already held.

In 1925 his doctoral advisor asked him to look at an unpublished paper by the young physicist Werner Heisenberg who was working on atomic theory. Dirac managed to unlock a deeper meaning from his work. Within months Dirac had written a paper entitled *The Fundamental Equations of Quantum Mechanics*. Three weeks after it was written, Dirac's paper was published by the Royal Society.

Dirac, although yet to complete his doctorate, began lecturing students and professors on quantum mechanics. He achieved his PhD in June 1926, just before his twenty-fourth birthday.

He left Cambridge to work in Copenhagen and Göttingen, publishing his radical *Quantum Theory of the Emission and Absorption of Radiation* in 1927. Before this, no theory accounted for the creation and annihilation of quantum objects such as photons. Before the end of the year Dirac had created the fundamental wave equation of the relativistic theory of the electron – the Dirac Equation.

Early in February 1928 the Royal Society published Dirac's *The Quantum Theory of the Electron*. Physicists worldwide were amazed; it is widely regarded as one of the greatest physics papers ever written. Among other things, the Dirac Equation predicted anti-matter, which scientists later discovered, naming the anti-electron 'Positron'. This is now used to detect cancers.

Dirac completed his book *The Principles of Quantum Mechanics* in 1930. It became the essential work for students of the subject and was even used as a reference by Einstein.

Dirac's annual lectures at Cambridge between 1930 and 1933 were legendary. In 1933 he and Schrödinger shared the Nobel Prize for Physics for their discovery of atomic theory. Dirac's work influenced scientists during his life and continues to do so to this day.

Dirac hated publicity, was reluctant to accept the Nobel Prize, and turned down other honours including a knighthood. In 1969 he moved to the United States, where he engaged in research at the University of Miami and Florida State University and died in Tallahassee, Florida, in October 1984, aged eighty-two.

# Downs

Clifton and Durdham Downs cover over 400 acres and were once the common land belonging to the manors of Clifton and Henbury. They were rough pasture, used for sheep grazing, studded with gorse bushes and to walk through this lonely landscape might well have been a less than pleasant experience, certainly best avoided when daylight faded. There were reports of robbers attacking travellers, even holding up coaches, and the victims didn't always escape with their lives.

The sheep grazing became less important as the eighteenth century progressed. There had been quarrying and mining for quite a while but now this activity increased as more new houses and roads were being built. The open quarries presented a hazard for the unwary. In 1833 a letter to the newspaper remarked on the exposed and dangerous state of the quarry between the Sea Walls and the Stoke Bishop Road, which 'without any kind of fence presents a precipice of 20 feet'.

Flowering trees on the Downs.

View across the Downs – the uneven surface is due to extensive stone quarrying in the past.

Such things didn't put off those who came to the Downs for sporting activities. Annual horse races were held, offering valuable prizes for the winners. There were also wrestling and boxing contests, foot races and cricket matches plus the occasional cockfight.

The spread of houses right to the edge of the Downs rang alarm bells, as there were reports of encroachments. The Clifton and Durdham Downs Act 1861 received royal assent and, stating how this land had 'from time immemorial been open and largely resorted to as places of recreation for the inhabitants of Bristol', this status must be maintained. Not only that, there was to be a committee which would stringently oversee everything.

So the quarries were gradually filled in and trees were planted – some in clumps, some in avenues, some as single specimens to mark special occasions. There are many varieties from the holly and hawthorn to beech, birch, whitebeam and oak and it is worth following the Tree Trail from Christchurch, Clifton, to look at some of them.

# Drinking Fountains

In November 2018 Bristol City Council announced that in order to reduce the use of disposable plastic bottles, they were planning to introduce a number of new public drinking fountains across the city in a scheme that would hopefully restore some historic fountains that have fallen into disuse. Public drinking fountains were mentioned as coming into vogue in an 1857 Bristol newspaper and a couple of years later the council was debating what the city should do about the idea. One councillor stated that it was 'the duty of society to provide for its members to be sober and economical', the alternative obviously being seen as people going off to slake their thirst at beerhouses.

Many fountains were set up during the nineteenth and early twentieth centuries, paid for by various benefactors and in various settings, so some designs were far more elaborate than others. With the automatic supply of piped water to buildings in the city, the fountains were seen as redundant and mechanisms were disabled. Now they may come into their own again.

*Above*: Coalbrookdale-made Queen Victoria Memorial Drinking Fountain, St Nicholas Street, erected 1859.

*Right*: Simon Short Memorial Fountain in Trinity Place, Hotwells.

TRINITY PLACE

# E

## Edward III

Although Henry III had permitted Bristol 'to choose a mayor after the manner of London', over 150 years later his great-grandson Edward III granted more important rights. In 1373 the Great Charter of Liberties stated that the town 'henceforth be separate from the counties of Gloucester and Somerset … and that it should be a county by itself, to be called the County of Bristol'. This was in response to a petition from the mayor and people, setting forward, among other things, the difficulties of travelling to the courts in Gloucester and Ilchester for assizes and inquests. Now Bristol would be able to have its own courts to dispense justice.

During Edward's reign there was constant war with France and Bristol ships had been among his forces, while the taxes paid by the merchants of the town had contributed greatly to fund the never-ending conflict. The charter could be seen as recognition for services rendered by loyal subjects in awarding privilege and status, but the royal gift came with a price. Edward's coffers were by now dangerously depleted and 600 marks were handed over to seal the granting of the charter.

## Electricity House

Electricity House was built between Lewins Mead and Rupert Street on the site of the demolished Demerara House, the frontage of which bore the 'left-handed giant' figurehead of the ill-fated SS *Demerara*. The *Demerara* was a mail steam packet built in Bristol by William Patterson. Her launching in 1851 was marred by the fact that as she was floated out of dock one of the retaining structures malfunctioned, striking the ship and delaying her entry into the harbour.

This was nothing compared to the disaster after she left the harbour and set off downriver, towed by a tug, a little too fast in people's opinion. After passing the sharp double turn of Round Point the bow struck rocks. The tide was on the ebb and she was violently strained and twisted, so she buckled. Despite valiant efforts there was nothing that could be done to save her and she had to be broken up for scrap.

*Above left*: A small replica of the Demerara figurehead on the Drawbridge pub in St Augustine's Parade.

*Above right*: Electricity House and the Cenotaph.

When Demerara House was demolished the figurehead disintegrated and could not be saved. On the front of the Drawbridge pub there is a smaller-sized replica that gives some idea of the original.

Electricity House was designed in the 1930s for the Electricity Board by Sir Giles Gilbert Scott as a showroom and offices complete with underground car park. Sleek, unornamented and of white Portland stone, this was a beacon of modernity. The Second World War intervened and in 1940, with the shell of the building complete but before being fitted out internally, it was requisitioned for aircraft construction. It was not completed until around 1950 but since then the elegant rounded shape has been a landmark of the area. No longer used as offices, it has been converted to apartments.

# F

## Floating Harbour

Bristol was almost encircled by the rivers Avon and Frome. The Frome had been diverted in 1240, when the old harbour was no longer adequate, by digging the 'great trench' of St Augustine's Reach. This had created a new area of quayside for loading and unloading of cargoes.

As vessels had got larger, the Avon had increasingly become a problem with its winding approach to the port. However, very importantly, there was around 30-foot difference between high and low tide, the second highest in the world. Ships in harbour rose and fell, restricting the loading and unloading times. As the eighteenth century progressed, the harbour was criticised as being crowded and inefficient because the ships were kept there far longer than necessary due to the harbour's tidal nature. Something had to be done to keep ships afloat all the time.

In the 1750s William Champion had suggested the idea of damming the river to create a section that was maintained at a more or less constant water level. There were frequent quibbles about the rights and wrongs of interfering with the system as

Entrance to Bristol Docks in the early 1900s showing P&A Campbell paddle steamer.

it stood. It wasn't until 1802 that the fledgling Bristol Dock Company engaged William Jessop, a noted engineer, to take the matter in hand. By the time it was finished the cost had almost doubled from Jessop's estimate at this time.

Following his designs, basically the river was dammed with locks in two places – at Cumberland Basin and near Temple Meads. This created a Floating Harbour, a section of river that allowed ships to permanently float without risk of grounding on the bottom. The remainder of the river flowed into the New Cut, a channel dug by hundreds of navvies. It was a large and challenging project, which wasn't completed until 1809 at a total cost of £600,000.

Did this price include the cost for the dinner to which the Bristol Dock directors treated the labourers employed on the canal and docks in celebration of the completion of the Floating Harbour? It was set out in a field between the harbour and the New Cut where around 1,000 workmen sat down to dinner watched by a host of spectators. It was a real feast consisting of two whole oxen, six hundredweight of plum pudding, bread and potatoes and 1,000 gallons of ale.

It was no doubt the ale that did it. When a cart arrived with fresh supplies an argument broke out between the English and the Irish navvies as to who was going to get refills first. The resulting battle raged down to Marsh Street, where many of the Irish lodged. Things got really violent, broken up only by the arrival of constables and the press gang, though no one was actually killed.

Jessop's plan worked but there were problems with the harbour silting up. Brunel was approached for a possible solution in 1832. He designed a series of sluices, known as the Underfall, as well as a special dredger known as a 'dragboat', which kept the harbour as silt-free as possible using its scraper blade. In the end it was only a temporary respite as the facilities could not cope with progress to steamships.

St Augustine's Reach.

New docks were built at Avonmouth to handle larger vessels although the City Docks continued to function in a small way until the 1960s.

After the docks were closed to commercial traffic, the Floating Harbour could have been filled in if the powers that be had had their way. It took much determination and a long fight, but now the harbour is a focus for leisure activities and the setting for housing developments, both purpose-built or conversions from a variety of old dockside buildings.

*Above*: Floating Harbour by Pooles Wharf.

*Left*: Boats at Bristol Harbour Festival.

# G

## Graffiti

Graffiti has come a long way from the old dictionary definition of 'rude drawings and personal sentiments scribbled on the walls of buildings'. The game changer was the development of spray paints. See it as defacement or enhancement, political statement, social comment or humorous observation, Bristol has many examples and some are now world-famous.

Because of the very nature of what they do, many street artists keep a strict anonymity, using a nickname as their signature. One of the most well-known is

Decorative written graffiti.

*Left*: Well Hung Lover
– graffiti seen from the
bottom of Park Street.

*Below*: Graffiti painting by
Skor85.

Banksy, who started way back in the last decades of the twentieth century and even staged an extensive exhibition at Bristol Museum in 2009. It was so popular that people queued for hours to get in.

# Grant, Cary

Cary Grant was a consummate actor, turning himself from the rebellious and scruffy Bristol schoolboy Archie Leach into a suave, sophisticated Hollywood film star. Born in Horfield in 1904, his home life was not a happy one. His mother suffered from depression and was overprotective as her first and only other child had died when

In 2001 this life-size bronze statue of Cary Grant, by Graham Ibbeson, was placed in Millennium Square.

young, while his father seems to have carried on a social life of his own. When he was eleven his mother suddenly disappeared from his life and he was told by his rather distant and unsympathetic father that she had gone on holiday and then died, when in fact she had been committed to Glenside Hospital and remained there.

After attending Bishop Road Junior School, he progressed to Fairfield Secondary School, but his lessons held little interest for him. What did was sparked by a visit to the new Hippodrome theatre in his teens with a teacher. He was hooked and spent much time working behind the scenes and on the lighting system there after school and no doubt even playing truant to do so. Here he fell in with the Pender touring comedy troupe and forged a letter of permission from his father to join them, but was hauled back to Bristol by his outraged parent when his absence was discovered. He didn't give up and when, in 1918, he was expelled from Fairfield for his behaviour, he took to the road with them.

In 1920 the Pender company went to America and toured there for two years. By then young Archie Leach had decided he was going to stay and graduated to proper acting, appearing in plays and musicals and then on Broadway. Hollywood was of course the place where real fame could be found and he was signed by Paramount Pictures, where his name was changed to Cary Grant, a name that appeared on over seventy films, from comedies to thrillers.

When his father died in 1935, Cary Grant learned for the first time that he had been lied to about his mother, that she was in fact still alive and in an institution for the mentally ill. He gained her release and over the years travelled to Bristol to visit her until she died nearly four decades later.

# SS *Great Britain*

Reduced to a hulk storing wood and coal, beached and rusting on the other side of the world, this is the ship that came back from the dead, to the very dock where she was built. The striking sight of SS *Great Britain* today, pennants fluttering from masts and funnels, is a testament not only to the original design and build but also to those who organised her remarkable return from the South Atlantic and then painstakingly restored her over the years since 1970.

The *Great Britain* was known as the *Mammoth Steamship*, designed by Isambard Kingdom Brunel and made of iron, when most large vessels, including battleships, were still constructed of wood; in fact she was longer by 100 feet than any battleship of the Royal Navy at that time. Up against the American supremacy in the North Atlantic trade, Brunel pulled out all the stops in her design from the innovative use of a screw propeller to accommodation for up to 360 passengers. It would be, it was said, a triumph for Bristol enterprise, Bristol capital and Bristol skill.

The initial construction was carried out in the Great Western Dry Dock and 19 July 1843 was the date arranged for the ship to be launched into the harbour and moved

Decorated stern of Brunel's SS *Great Britain*.

to Gas Works Wharf where engines and fittings would be installed. With the city decorated and the population in jubilant mood, Prince Albert arrived in a colourful cavalcade to the ringing of bells and discharge of cannon. The ship was then open for inspection by the public and proved a great attraction.

Unfortunately the addition of considerable weight from the engines had an effect that no one seems to have thought of. It meant that the *Great Britain*'s broadest part now floated lower in the water, so was too wide to pass through the exit lock from Cumberland Basin downriver to the sea. So unless something could be done to increase the size of that opening, she was trapped.

Relations between the Great Western Steamship Co., who owned the ship, and the Docks Company, who owned the lock, were sadly not good. For months the negotiations continued over what could be done and what would be allowed to be done. Eventually Brunel received permission to modify the entrance, but even then it was a squeeze as it took the highest tide to give just enough lift to set the *Great Britain* free on 11 December 1844.

Of course, because of her size, it was obvious that she would never be able to use Bristol as a port and her transatlantic voyages were from Liverpool. The Liverpool–New York runs took between thirteen and twenty days but were not always straightforward, with engine troubles and a grounding off Ireland. Later, in 1852, after major alterations, the ship was transferred to the Melbourne run, bringing back gold from the Ballarat goldfields to the value of more than £500,000 on one voyage alone. During the Crimean and Abyssinian Wars the ship was used as a troop carrier, sometimes laden with 1,500 men plus supplies, while smaller numbers of invalided soldiers were transported home on each return.

Put up for sale in 1876 and stripped of her engines, the *Great Britain* was demoted to a cargo-carrying sailing ship and damaged during a storm, so was put back to the Falkland Islands. By now she was considered not worthy of repair, so was beached and merely used for storage and later holed and abandoned. Who could imagine then that years later she would once more be a great attraction here in Bristol?

Prow of the SS *Great Britain*.

# High Cross

The four principal thoroughfares of mediaeval Bristol were High Street, Broad Street, Wine Street and Corn Street and where they joined stood the High Cross. It was made of carved stone, with niches containing statues of four kings who had conferred charters that had contributed to Bristol's trade growth – John, Henry III, Edward III and Edward IV.

Top section of the 1850 High Cross, now in Berkeley Square.

In 1633 the High Cross was repaired and altered to include the figures of Henry VI, Elizabeth, James I and Charles I, who had further endowed privileges on the city. At 39 feet tall, richly painted in vermilion, blue and gold, and surrounded by steps and an iron fence, it must have been an impressive sight.

A hundred years later, it was considered something of a 'superstitious relick', which was in a rather dangerous state and an obstacle to traffic, by people such as the deputy chamberlain Mr Vaughan. He lived at the corner of High and Wine Streets and claimed he feared for his life and property every time the wind blew around the it. Enough people agreed with him to get the High Cross put away in the Guildhall.

There were some protests about such treatment and the High Cross was re-erected on College Green. This became a popular place for the fashionable set to promenade in large groups, so the cross got in their way and in 1763, as it stood on land owned by the cathedral, it was removed to that building and deposited in a corner. A few years later it was given away by the Dean of Bristol to his friend Henry Hoare of Stourhead, to use as an estate ornament.

In 1850 a copy was made and erected on College Green. Nearly forty years on this was moved to a more central position and statues by the sculptor Harry Hems were added. It was not allowed to rest there in peace, however. In the mid-twentieth century the architect of the new Council House that was being built, fronting onto College Green, decided that the High Cross did not fit with his plans and it was banished once more, this time to a Corporation Yard where it was wantonly vandalised. Through an appeal by the Civic Society enough money was raised to restore the top part, which can be found in Berkeley Square, Clifton.

# Hills

Historians of the past tried hard to give Bristol a Roman pedigree but, unable to come up with anything positive, fell back on a seeming likeness to Rome, with claims that the Avon bends in a curve almost identical to that of the Tiber and that both cities are built on seven hills. Bristol is indeed a hilly city. Laurence Cowen, better known by his pen name of Lesser Columbus, described it as 'a most uneven sort of place. Every now and then its streets move heavenwards with a suddenness almost appalling'.

Lodge Street is quite short, running uphill alongside the Red Lodge, part of which dates back to Elizabethan times, and its garden. The roadway is still paved with cobbled stones.

When Park Street was built in the eighteenth century, it rose steeply from the old Frog Lane towards the lush grasslands of Bullocks Park where cattle grazed. It was a real pull for the horses and an extra two were usually added, when going up, to give increased power. The view over the city was splendid though and it was a very fashionable address. In 1871 a viaduct was constructed at the bottom to traverse Frogmore Street, as Frog Lane had become, and this somewhat reduced the severe

*Right*: Park Street from College Green.

*Below*: Looking down St Michael's Hill with St Michael's Church tower.

Brandon Hill with Cabot Tower.

starting gradient. By then some of the houses had been converted into shops, a trend that continued until the street became a high-class shopping destination.

St Michael's Hill was an important route out of Bristol for centuries, described on Millerd's 1673 map as the way to Aust Ferry and Wales. The church of St Michael is mentioned in late twelfth-century documents, although rebuilt later, suffered war damage, was rebuilt again, declared redundant in 1999, then ravaged by fire in 2016 and now hopefully to be restored. A few houses date from the 1630s, although most are from the 1700s developments and onwards. At the end of the road Bewell's Cross, also called Gallows Cross, stood in the Gallows Field at what was the boundary of the city. Executions took place there until 1816.

Horfield Road once was called Upper Maudlin Lane. In those days it came to the grassy area of the King's Down where Kingsdown Parade, Somerset Street and Dove Street were soon to be built. Parts of Kingsdown suffered from redevelopment in the 1960s but, in spite of all the destruction, fine examples of Georgian houses still survive.

If you make your way upwards on Brandon Hill's paths you can look out over Bristol. Climb the steps of the Cabot Tower perched on top and you really get a bird's-eye view that makes you appreciate how high above the old city you have reached in a relatively short distance.

# The Hotwell

The Hotwell isn't actually hot, but a tepid spring that started to gather popularity towards the end of the seventeenth century as a reputed cure for many endemic diseases. It was difficult to access until a Pump Room was built over it and then came 'a great influx of nobility and gentry from all places', as the guidebook of the time put it. Visiting spas had become fashionable and not just for those who were ill.

40

Engraving showing the old Hotwell House.

It wasn't only drinking the water of course; it was attending balls, going to musical entertainments, taking river trips and enjoying the scenery.

It didn't last, in spite of improvements that were made to keep the enterprise going. The truth was that many of the people who came desperate for a cure succumbed to their illness and belief in the water's efficacy lost credibility. Those who wanted to mix with society followed its leaders to more fashionable places. The Hotwell House was pulled down, although the Colonnade, built as shops, still stands. Today the spring is only visible at low tide but the name of Hotwells remains.

The Colonnade, Hotwells.

# Infirmary

The Bristol Royal Infirmary, as it became, was founded as long ago as 1736. John Elbridge, who had been comptroller of customs during the reign of William III, made a heartfelt plea to the citizens of Bristol 'as a remedy for the misery of our poor neighbours' by providing medical aid supported by voluntary contributions. Over seventy people signed up, agreeing to donate a few guineas, and enough subscriptions flowed in to buy a plot of land and then to set up a building by 1737. Elbridge himself died a couple of years later and left a bequest of £5,000 to the Infirmary in his will.

This first building only held twelve beds but was extended by adding wings to each side. Even with these additions it was cramped, with low ceilings and poor ventilation, and by the 1780s was hopelessly inadequate, so Thomas Paty, a local architect, was asked to supply plans for something that was purpose built, fronting onto Marlborough Street. Because of money constraints it was constructed in several phases but by 1814 it provided beds for 180 patients.

One surgeon whose service at the hospital stretched from 1796 to 1843 was Richard Smith. Over this period he collected many pathological specimens, which were later housed in a museum on the premises, for which he had left a sum of money.

The reputation of the hospital grew and Queen Victoria gave assent to the title Royal being added to its name in 1850. This was probably the same year when chloroform was first used in a BRI operation. As the century progressed new additions were made, including an outpatients' department and a nurses' home. However, an important change was made in 1911–12 when the King Edward VII Memorial Building was erected on the opposite side of Marlborough Street, which provided extra surgical wards.

A 1965 block next to the Edward VII Memorial Building was voted one of the ugliest buildings in Bristol and for years its concrete exterior presented a rather grim face. In 2012–13 an international competition was held for proposals to create a new and more welcoming facade. Six submissions were put forward in an international competition and a design named 'Veil' by Spanish architects Nieto

Bristol Royal Infirmary.

Sobejano was selected as the winner following a public vote and recommendation from the panel overseeing the competition. This now presents a more modern and energy-efficient exterior.

The Georgian building has been under threat for some time. No longer used since 2016, there were plans put forward to demolish it and replace it with accommodation for 715 people, in a building up to nine storeys tall. The old hospital has been seen as an important historic building and the conservation area has been extended to include it, but at present its future is in doubt.

# Jackson, Samuel

In the 1820s, '30s and '40s Samuel Jackson was a member of a group of Bristol-based artists. He was described as being modest, upright and friendly, enjoying music and playing the piano and guitar. He would go on sketching parties to the woods around the Avon Gorge with his artist friends, but whereas many of them went off elsewhere to make a living, Jackson continued to live and work in Bristol until he died.

Nightingale Valley, where Samuel Jackson and his friends went sketching.

He did travel extensively though, not only to the South West counties but to northern England, Wales, Scotland and even the West Indies and, late in his life, to Switzerland.

He was commissioned to paint pictures of Brunel's design submissions for the Clifton Suspension Bridge in 1830 and of the approved design when work was about to start in 1836. Although he produced drawings and paintings of imaginary landscapes, exhibited in London, his great skill was in rendering accomplished, crisp and luminous watercolour views depicting Bristol streetscapes, the harbour and the gorge. They provide a striking contrast to the black and white harshness of similar scenes in photographs only a few years later.

Several of his paintings are in the Braikenridge Collection in the Bristol Museum and Art Gallery. G. W. Braikenridge was a local antiquarian who commissioned artists such as Jackson, James Johnson and T. L. Rowbotham to draw various views of the Bristol landscape during the 1820s. Thus was preserved an invaluable detailed record of the city just before Victorian development took a hold.

# James, Thomas

There was ever a rivalry between Bristol and London merchants. In the 1600s the search was still on for a way to the Orient by sailing west and when Bristol's Merchant Venturers learned that their London counterparts were sending a ship to find a north-west passage through, they scrambled to equip a vessel of their own with all speed. The able navigator they chose as their captain was Thomas James and he sailed out on the *Henrietta Maria* in May 1631.

He arrived in June near Davis Strait, where he encountered ice and for several weeks fought his way through it into Hudson Bay. He finally reached land on 11 August. He did meet up with Foxe, the London merchants' captain, who was apparently not impressed with this rival and they went their separate ways. After a short period of exploration, James realised that due to storms and ice he was not going to find a way through and he and his crew would have to overwinter, so built cabins on Charlton Island.

The Canadian winter took its toll. Their clothing wasn't warm enough to cope with the extreme cold and their provisions were woefully inadequate. They not only grew weak but suffered from scurvy and four men died. Those that made it through to warm weather then found themselves plagued by mosquitoes. They recommenced their efforts to find the passage through, reaching 65 degrees 30 N with no success. Realising they had to leave before ice completely blocked their way once more, James abandoned his search and limped back home to Bristol, arriving in October 1632.

Thomas James wrote a detailed account of his expedition, which was very popular. Even though his mission had failed, Foxe's mission hadn't been successful either, so at least his rival had not beaten him. James died around three years after returning and one wonders how much this was due to the harsh conditions experienced by the expedition.

# K

## King Street

Probably the most evocative street in Bristol, King Street gives a flavour of what things were like in 'the old days'. It was named for King Charles II and there are houses here dating from his time. The Llandoger Trow with its timbered front and overhanging eaves is made up of several houses, though originally occupied only one.

Llandoger Trow in King Street.

The flat-bottomed boats called trows sailed across from towns like Llandogo in Wales, mooring to unload their goods in nearby Welsh Back.

The Old Duke was originally called the Duke of Cumberland after the son of George II, who defeated Bonnie Prince Charlie at Culloden and then ordered his troops to systematically hunt down the Highlanders. Duke Ellington is the face on the signboard now and the pub is renowned for live jazz and blues music.

*Above*: King Street towards Welsh Back, showing the Old Duke.

*Right*: General view of King Street.

St Nicholas' Almshouses were begun in 1652 and a bastion of the old city wall is visible in their courtyard. At the other end of the street are the Merchant Venturers' Almshouses of the later seventeenth century, which were built for retired sailors. Neither still function for their original purpose, the accommodation not considered suitable for modern pensioners.

The Georgian Theatre Royal, incorporating the Coopers Hall, presents a columned and pedimented exterior with recent redevelopment at the side to allow easier access. It has a long tradition of theatrical activity, opening in the 1760s, although not considered entirely respectable by some of those who lived in the neighbourhood at that time. Edmund Kean, Sarah Siddons and Ellen Terry performed there in its heyday but by the 1930s its productions featured mainly melodramas and revues. Fortunately it became home to the Bristol Old Vic Theatre Company after the Second World War, bringing many excellent and world-famous actors to its stage. Now it produces a wide variety of works in this theatre complex, from Shakespeare to experimental genres.

City wall bastion in the courtyard of St Nicholas' Almshouses.

# L

## Leonard Lane

To walk along this narrow lane is to follow the line of a section of old town wall from Small Street to where the church of St Leonard stood in Corn Street. This church with its bell tower was built over one of the town gates, which became known as St Leonard's Gate. Vaulted cellars for storage stretched right under Leonard Lane because that roadway and the churchyard were around 10 feet higher than the quayside outside the wall.

Leonard Lane looking toward the Small Street entrance.

The church and gate caused a constriction to the increased traffic of Georgian times. In 1766 it was reported in the Bishop of Bristol's diocese book that the parish of St Leonard was united with that of St Nicholas and the church and vicarage house were to be taken down to allow the construction of Clare Street, which joined the old city to the quayside area. There is a worn stone head over the entrance to the lane. Perhaps it is a lonely remnant of the demolished church.

# Light Vessel 55 – the John Sebastian

A light vessel is equipped with a warning beacon on a tall mast and anchored off the coast as an alert to hazards for sailors. *Light Vessel 55*, a Bristol-built wooden ship from the boatyard of Charles Hill, served in various waters off the British Isles, including the North Sea and the Bristol Channel, for nearly seventy years.

Eventually discarded as having passed any worthwhile use, the ship was sold for scrap and consequently more or less pulled apart. In a semi-burned and near derelict state the vessel was acquired by the Cabot Sailing Club in 1954. Moored in Bathurst Basin, the *John Sebastian* then underwent substantial repair and conversion into a headquarters for the club, which it still is today.

*Light Vessel 55, the John Sebastian.*

# M

## M Shed

From the outside M Shed may look rather unprepossessing and totally unlike a traditional museum but that is because it was once cargo transit shed M on the dockside. The size and functionality of the large space within makes it possible to show the history of Bristol in a more unconstrained way.

No longer required once the wharf had closed to commercial traffic, the building became the Industrial Museum, the home of important relics of Bristol's industrial past. Many of these were very large, connected with transport and aviation, and the museum was extremely popular, giving a chance of close encounters with the exhibits.

*Below left*: Entrance to M Shed Museum.

*Below right*: Fairbairn Steam Crane on the quayside near M Shed.

Steam locomotive Henbury on Bristol Harbour Railway outside M Shed.

The Industrial Museum closed in 2006 so that it could improve and upgrade to become the Museum of Bristol, having acquired grants for that purpose. You can still ring the bell on an old Bristol bus and marvel at giant aero engines but also learn about the growth of Bristol and hear stories of its people. There are exhibits outside too, which can often be seen working at weekends, including the steam and electric cranes and Harbour Railway engines.

# Markets

Traders originally set up their market stalls in High Street and Broad Street but this was increasingly viewed as an obstruction to both wheeled traffic and pedestrians. When the Exchange for merchants was planned in the 1740s and a site was cleared for it, a piece of this land was allocated to build a covered market around an open square. So the Glass Arcade was originally an open avenue but in the nineteenth century wooden stalls were fitted and a glazed roof installed.

The Exchange, to John Wood of Bath's design, featured colonnaded walkways around a square courtyard, which the Bristol merchants said they preferred for meeting and conducting business. This grand new building was greeted with pomp and ceremony on 21 September 1743, but later generations were less happy about the lack of roof and one was added. The Bristol corn market was held here and so it became known as the Corn Exchange and it was under that name in the 1960s that it became a music venue, played in by many of the popular groups of the time. Nowadays the Exchange Hall is a constituent part of St Nicholas Market.

Variety is the spice of life and variety is certainly on offer in this indoor market. There are flowers and fruit, jewellery and textiles, all sorts of unusual gifts and hobby items plus food stalls and cafés to suit every taste. St Nicholas Market itself is open

*Above left*: The Glass Arcade, St Nicholas Market.

*Above right*: A corner of the Exchange market.

*Below*: Corn Street flea market.

every day but there are other outdoor markets associated with it that are held weekly in Corn Street on specific days such as the Farmers' Market, the Street Food Market and the Saturday Nails Market.

It seems that the idea of the weekly street market is coming back into fashion in Bristol, generally on Saturdays. Examples can be found in Whiteladies Road, by the Watershed and at Finzel's Reach, while some are held on a less frequent but regular basis.

## Matthew

John Cabot was born in Genoa, later moving to Venice where he lived for around fifteen years when not at sea. He came to England looking to find financial backing for a voyage across the Atlantic, at the end of which he was sure he would reach the fabled lands of the East with their silks and spices. He settled in Bristol with his wife Mattea and three sons and petitioned Henry VII for royal backing to make this voyage.

In 1495 he received the hoped-for letters patent from the king. This document authorised Cabot and his three sons,

> to sail and take possession in the King's name of any unknown heathen or infidel lands they might discover, in consequence of which they were to render to the King in goods or money one-fifth of the net profits and gains of the voyage on their return to Bristol, with which port alone they were to trade. Other persons presuming to traffic with the regions were to forfeit all ships and merchandise.

Bronze sculpture of John Cabot by Stephen Joyce on Narrow Quay.

Now Bristol merchants could be persuaded to provide the money.

His first effort ended in a rather humiliating return to Bristol when, already short of supplies, he ran into bad weather. In 1497 he sailed once more in a ship called the *Matthew*, and this time arrived not in some warm Oriental paradise, but off the rather chilly coast of Newfoundland. The ship sailed back to Bristol and Cabot was given a pension of five pounds by the king. He then seems to disappear from history although his son Sebastian made a couple more expeditions but not in the *Matthew*, which returned to working on normal trade routes.

No one really knows what Cabot's ship looked like but the crew only numbered twenty at most. When a replica *Matthew* was constructed in the 1990s, to celebrate the 500th anniversary of the voyage, it surprised people to realise how small the vessel would have been. Based on detailed studies of old drawings and plans of Tudor ships backed by archaeological evidence, the *Matthew* that sailed over to Newfoundland and back in 1997 is a mere 78 feet long. Standing on the deck you can only marvel at the thought of this wooden ship tossed on the Atlantic waves.

The Matthew of Bristol, a modern replica of John Cabot's ship.

# N

## The Nails

In Corn Street, in front of the Exchange, stand four bronze pillars known as the Nails, which were removed in 1771 from the Tolzey where the merchants used to meet. One had been there as long ago as 1550 and is very worn. They were used as payment tables, document rests, apparently even to lean on, as they were in an outdoor space with no seating, but they gave rise to the saying 'paying on the nail' to mean immediate payment.

All the Nails are slightly different in design. The inscription on one tells that it was the gift of a merchant named Robert Kitchen who had been mayor and alderman. Another, dating from 1631, was given by George White, 'brother unto Dr Thomas White, a famous benefactor to this citie'. In 1625 a plague epidemic swept the country but got no further than the eastern gate of the city. Because of this deliverance, Nicholas Crisp was the grateful donor of a Nail bearing words of thanks beginning,

The Nail donated by Nicholas Crisp.

'Prais the Lord O my soule, and forget not all his benefits. He saved my life from destruction', on which the maker, Thomas Hobson, also inscribed his own name.

# Neptune

Neptune first appeared on the Bristol streets in 1723, made of lead by Joseph Rendall, although the actual sculptor who designed him is unknown. This larger-than-life-size painted statue decorated the newly renovated Temple conduit, a place to which spring water was piped for the use of the inhabitants. He was moved after sixty odd years for a short stay outside some almshouses, but was then 'hidden in a corner near Temple Church'.

The 1870s brought him back into the limelight, after 'suffering the rude buffeting of ages' according to a newspaper article of the time, ready to become 'a striking ornament to Victoria Street'. This involved more than just a quick scrub and brush up. Even before work could begin Mr Lawrence, the renovator, had to make some drastic alterations to his workshop by cutting away part of the doorway and raising its roof to accommodate such a large item. In 1872 Neptune was set on an 11-foot-high pedestal so he could be admired by all who passed to and from the railway station.

There have been two more moves since. One in 1949 placed him on the Bridgehead on the Centre with his back to St Augustine's Reach. Towards the end of the twentieth century structural repairs were necessary and, with the millennium changes to the Centre, he was moved to the middle of the reorganised area as though looking towards the Floating Harbour. He cuts perhaps a fatherly rather than a kingly figure, unrelentingly grey in colour now, but loved by Bristolians for all that.

Neptune in his present location on the Centre.

# The Normans

Bristol as a place of settlement and trade certainly existed in the tenth century because it was briefly mentioned then in the Anglo-Saxon Chronicle and coins minted in Bristol for later Saxon kings have been found. It was the Normans, however, who put their stamp on the place. They saw its strategic importance as the site for a castle, their way of keeping control over hostile territory they had invaded.

There doesn't seem to have been any significant resistance in the Bristol area, no recorded skirmishes further south-west, no legendary heroes like Hereward the Wake carrying out guerrilla raids further east. In fact, when the dead King Harold's sons landed only a year after the battle of Hastings, hoping to rouse the country to rebellion, the men of Bristol apparently defended the town against them and drove them off.

The original castle was quite small, of the motte-and-bailey design, but it was rebuilt and enlarged by various phases of construction. The Great Keep was built on the instructions of the powerful Robert, Earl of Gloucester, illegitimate son of Henry I, and an old poem tells of this 'nobel toure, that of all the towers in England is said to be the floure'. There are no contemporary drawings of the castle, although what is said to be its water gate is shown on the Bristol coat of arms. The earliest illustration seems to have been made in the seventeenth century probably just before the castle's destruction, when the Corporation of Bristol, with the authority of Oliver Cromwell, pulled it down.

To them this was an outdated crumbling eyesore and the ideal thing was to get rid of it and use the land for high-quality houses. You can still see a section of the base of the Norman keep, a couple of rooms that were probably porches and used later as shops (which miraculously survived the blitz), some retaining walls and the sally port entrance.

What is certain is that the castle's useful life was mostly during the Norman period. As well as building the Great Keep, Robert, Earl of Gloucester gave land and materials for the erection of the Benedictine Priory of St James in the Barton just down the hill, outside the town. The west front of St James' Church features an interlaced arcade and a wheel window and inside are massive stone pillars, all typical of Norman architecture.

It was another Robert, Robert Fitzharding, the 1st Lord Berkeley, who founded the Abbey of St Augustine in 1142. The Dissolution of the Monasteries swept away many abbey buildings but notably preserved its collegiate church to become Bristol Cathedral. The vaulted chapter house however is a fine example of the spare Norman style and the archway of what was the abbey gatehouse has similar decoration.

Across College Green is the Lord Mayor's Chapel, St Mark's, originally the chapel of the Hospital of the Gaunts, which was founded in 1220 by Maurice de Gaunt to be an almonry of the abbey. A further later endowment from his nephew established an independent religious community, known as the bons-hommes, who helped the poor. Inside the chapel there are two blank-faced stone effigies lying side by side, which are reputed to be Maurice de Gaunt and his nephew. Clad in chain mail and carrying a kite shield, they look just like the Norman soldiers who took possession of Bristol after the Battle of Hastings.

*Above left*: The west front of the Priory Church of St James.

*Above right*: The Norman Arch, St Augustine's Gateway on College Green.

*Right*: Stone effigy of Maurice de Gaunt in the Lord Mayor's Chapel.

# O'Brien – the Irish Giant

It was 1779 when, the story goes, William Watts, a hosier who lived at No. 24 High Street, went to visit a friend who was in the debtors' gaol (known colloquially as the sponging house) in Tailor's Court. On entering the building, his ears were assailed by a loud howling noise that was coming from an extremely tall Irishman hunched up miserably in a space never meant to accommodate his 8-foot-plus height. Watts learned that the young man, Patrick Cotter, had been brought over to Bristol on a ship that traded with Ireland, by a man looking to make money by exhibiting him in a freak show. But as they disagreed over payment, the man had sworn out a debt upon him, so he had been locked up as unable to pay.

Mr Watts was apparently not one to miss an opportunity, especially as he knew the fair was coming up, so he bailed him out and speedily had a red coat and waistcoat trimmed with gold plus a large gold-laced hat made to fit his protégé. Then the drawing room at a pub called the Jolly Brewers was fitted out, displaying a banner reading, 'The Irish Giant, the lineal descendant of the old and puissant King Brian Boru. Near nine feet high.' Patrick had the surname O'Brien added to his name, to reinforce the emblazoned relationship to the ancient king.

Crowds flocked to see him and by the end of the fair it's said he was given a golden guinea. He handed this over to Mr Watts on condition that he was engaged for every future fair and that the Jolly Brewers should change its name to the Giant's Castle. He then began to exhibit himself at fairs and theatres in London and other places, accumulating a great deal of money and buying a carriage that he used for his travels as well as a couple of houses in Kingsdown. He considered Bristol his home and he 'regularly of an afternoon took his pipe at the Artichoke and the Ben Johnson Porter House under the Bank'.

It is said he enjoyed attending plays at the theatre and, a mild-mannered and amiable man, invariably sat with his back against the wall so as not to block the view of others. Along with the stories of his beginnings in showmanship, it's not always clear how much the truth has been embellished. His friendship with Mr Watts though seems to have continued to the time of his death in 1804 at the age of forty-six.

O'Brien had been retired for a couple of years by then, his large size contributing to weakness in his limbs. He bequeathed money to Mr Watts on the condition that he kept his body from falling into the hands of doctors who were always eager to dissect people displaying unusual traits. His remains were buried 12 feet down before the inner entrance door of the Roman Catholic chapel in Trenchard Street, fastened down by iron cramps in a piece of rock hollowed out to hold the extra-long coffin.

# P

## Pero

When the young Pero was purchased by John Pinney for his Nevis plantation, British ships had been involved in the slave trade for a century or more. The Bristol-born merchant Edward Colston became a member and later an official of the Royal African Company, which had been founded in 1672. This London company had a monopoly of the trade with the coast of West Africa, not only in gold and silver but in transporting slaves over to the plantations of North America and the Caribbean.

The Georgian House, Great George Street. Here the enslaved Pero was servant to John Pinney.

This Bridge, designed by Eilis O'Connell, was opened in 1999 and named in honour of Pero.

In 1698 that monopoly was overturned and many Bristol merchants now employed their ships in what they saw as a lucrative field of operations. This was a triangular trade with ships setting out for West African ports with iron and brass goods, guns and cloth, exchanging them there for native men and women, snatched from their homes, who could be sold as slaves and then returning back across the North Atlantic to Bristol with holds full of sugar, rum, molasses, tobacco and so on. The slaves were treated as cargo rather than as people, so they were kept below decks for the voyage, chained and ill-fed.

Pero Jones became the property of John Pinney to work at Mountravers as a house slave in 1765 and later was his personal servant. When Pinney returned to Bristol after around twenty years Pero came with him, but was never given his freedom. He travelled back to Nevis a couple of times and Pinney noticed that after the second visit 'he has not conducted himself as well as I could have wished'. Pero became ill and was sent to Ashton for a change of air but sadly never recovered.

# Plimsoll, Samuel

Samuel Plimsoll was born in Bristol in 1824 and although he and his family moved away when he was quite young, he developed a strong interest in the privations suffered by seamen on ships operated by unscrupulous shipowners. These so-called 'coffin ships' were poorly maintained and grossly overloaded but heavily insured. As an MP he campaigned for a safe load line to be painted on all ships, antagonising many owners of merchant vessels who said the Board of Trade regulations were adequate.

He carefully recorded reports of ships which sank and published a book called *Our Seamen*, setting out his views, visiting various ports, holding meetings in connection with this. An evening public meeting in Bristol in June 1873 was attended by 3,000 people after he had been accompanied through the streets in the afternoon by Royal Naval Reserve men, shipwrights, boiler makers and sailors. Three years later it seemed as though all his work had been successful when a government bill was introduced, only for it to be dropped.

Plimsoll exploded angrily in Parliament with a violent diatribe, shaking his fist at the Speaker and with threats of a reprimand hanging over him, then had to apologise. A swelling tide of support for him and his cause began flowing from the public, expressed in newspapers and at meetings. It meant the government had to take notice, resulting in the passing of the Merchant Shipping Act, which brought in some stringent new regulations. One of these was the requirement for an indicator on the side of each ship showing the maximum depth to which that ship might be legally loaded. It's known, in honour of the man who worked so hard for such improvements, as the Plimsoll Line.

Bust of Samuel Plimsoll, originally located on Hotwell Road, has been re-erected at Capricorn Quay, Harbourside.

# Q

## Quakers

The Society of Friends, or Quakers, had an important influence on Bristol trade and commerce but for a while in the seventeenth century they were very much a persecuted section of the community. After Charles II was restored to the throne the bishops were restored to Parliament and several Acts were passed that brought in harsh repressive religious controls that penalised Nonconformist groups, including the Quakers. These included closing down their meeting houses, as no more than four people were allowed to meet in a house for worship.

Denis Hollister, a prominent Quaker, had purchased a site originally belonging to a Dominican order of friars. Even a hundred years and more after the order had been dissolved by Henry VIII, local people still called this place by their name. So when

Buildings from the Dominican Friary.

a meeting house was erected on this land, the congregation were referred to as 'the Quakers at the Friars', which became shortened to Quakers Friars. During the time of intolerance there could be no worship there and in fact it was attacked and damaged. Secretive services were held in the fields and woods just over the river in Gloucestershire.

With the Act of Toleration of 1687 religious liberties were restored to Nonconformists and Quakers gained a reputation as sober, respectable and hard-working members of society. Although William Penn's colony in America attracted some to cross the ocean, other Quakers carried on a variety of trades in Bristol from shoemakers to pewterers, distillers to tailors, bakers to glaziers and owners of influential eighteenth-century local newspapers, like Sarah Farley, Samuel Bonner and Thomas Middleton. There were those who became extremely successful in their business, like the Goldneys with interests in banking, shipping and iron and brass manufacture, and the Frys, a household name for chocolate.

Quakers were at the forefront of social concerns and humanitarian campaigns including prison reform and the abolition of the slave trade. As early as 1696 they had founded a workhouse for poor weavers in St Jude's, which produced woollen cloth. The Quakers Friars' meeting house was rebuilt in 1747 in a more open and airy galleried style and was used for around 200 years before members moved to a new 1962 building sited on the former burial ground of the old workhouse.

The old Friends' Meeting House at Quakers Friars.

# Queen Square

Looking at Queen Square today it's difficult to imagine it as a boggy area of long grass and reeds, home to ducks and wildfowl and known as the Marsh, though the nearby Marsh Street may give a clue. Some of the land was drained, part of it made into a bowling green, although John Evans wrote in his history of Bristol that other parts 'had long been used as a receptacle for the rubbish of the city'. Then as the seventeenth century drew to a close, it was decided that this would make a splendid site for new housing, which would supply the town council with a steady income from the ground rents they could charge.

With each side of the square measuring over 170 yards, this ambitious project was supposed to follow strict rules as to materials and dimensions to be used, so the buildings would harmonise together. Unfortunately, as there were several different architects and builders, the idea of a grand overall design failed, though these were looked on as prestigious dwellings by the merchants and shipowners who moved into them. When the nineteenth century came around it might have been more fashionable to reside in Clifton but Queen Square was a very respectable address to have.

In 1831 the square was fixed firmly in the spotlight of radical and violent civil disturbance. It started with anger at remarks made by Sir Charles Wetherell, the Recorder of Bristol, that Bristolians were against Parliamentary reform, which was the current political hot topic. He was in the city to preside over the Assizes and the crowds made it obvious when he opened the proceedings that their mood was aggressive. The Mansion House, the official residence of the mayor, was in the north-east corner of Queen Square and it was there that the Recorder always attended an official banquet in his honour.

A mob filled the square, shouting abuse and throwing stones. As there was no official police force at that time – just special constables who might have been

View of two sides of Queen Square.

handy with their bludgeons but had no disciplined training – nothing much could be done to stop them. The Recorder, the mayor and the other official dignitaries rushed into the Mansion House and as the hours passed the situation developed dramatically. The mayor read the Riot Act with no effect and, as many constables had left, a serious attack on the Mansion House began, smashing window sashes and shutters, then forcing the doors to surge in on the lower floor, splintering furniture and fittings.

Two divisions of Dragoon Guards under command of Colonel Brereton arrived and managed to restore some kind of order. They left in the morning, whereupon the crowd reformed and made an assault on the Mansion House cellars to avail themselves of the hundreds of bottles of wine stored there. The drunken looting then escalated and during the night the north-west side of the square was sacked and burnt, including the Mansion House and the Customs House as well as private dwellings. Some of the rioters were so drunk they perished in the flames.

What ended it was actual cavalry charges by soldiers 'done at the gallop and with the sword', according to one who took part in them. No one has ever managed to come up with an exact number of those killed and wounded during the affair. The official figure of deaths from the riot was twelve, with ninety-four injured, but that was those taken to hospitals. Many with wounds would have tried to get elsewhere rather than answer awkward questions. Looted items were found all over the city and apparently at least one cask of stolen brandy was poured down the sink.

New houses were built to replace those that had been destroyed, but in the 1930s an Inner Circuit road was constructed, so a broad carriageway was slashed diagonally through the middle of the square and the corner houses were demolished. It took over fifty years to right that wrong but traffic has now been banned from the central section and the old walkways restored.

J. M. Rysbrach's Bronze equestrian statue of King William III shows him dressed as a Roman emperor.

# R

## Raja Rammohun Roy

At almost 6 feet tall, Raja Rammohun Roy must have appeared an imposing figure in his Indian homeland but, clad in flowing robes, even more exotically so when he arrived in nineteenth-century Britain. Born into a Brahmin family in West Bengal around 1780, he was well travelled from boyhood, visiting various places for his

This life-size statue by Niranjan Sarkar was placed between City Hall and the cathedral in 1997.

education, with an interest in different religions as well as languages. He learned Persian, Arabic and Sanskrit and spent time in Tibet. He studied Greek writings by Aristotle and Euclid and taught himself English.

After his father died in the early 1800s, he became heir to a large amount of property and published a book in Persian condemning idolatry in religion. In 1814 he went to Calcutta and began studying English in earnest, both written and spoken. At the same time he translated the Vedas from the ancient Sanskrit into vernacular languages used by the Hindus and Bengalese.

While working for the East India Company, he developed a strong interest in the country's social issues. He set about providing education for others, establishing and maintaining native schools, promoting the study of scientific and mathematical subjects. He also challenged some of the Hindu traditions and superstitions which he considered anathema to civilised people. One of these was the practice of sati, where a widow was expected to throw herself on her dead husband's burning funeral pyre. He called this 'cruel murder, under the cloak of religion' and spent years in the campaign to stamp it out.

He had long wanted to visit Britain and was pleased to come as a representative of Indian views, arriving in Liverpool in April 1831. Not only did he meet members of parliament and take part in hearings and debates, but spent considerable time with reformers, scholars and religious leaders, among them the Unitarian Bristol minister Lant Carpenter and his daughter, Mary. His schedule was quite taxing and over two years it all took a toll on his health. By October 1833 he was quite exhausted and he came to stay at Stapleton Grove near Bristol, where he died of meningitis. He was buried in the grounds there, but in 1843 he was reburied at Arnos Vale Cemetery, in a grand tomb created in the style of a Bengali funeral monument.

# Redcliff(e)

At the time when Bristol was expanding by the Norman castle another settlement, called Redcliff, was growing up just across the river on land that belonged to the manor of Bedminster, owned by the Lords of Berkeley. The men of Redcliff used the river as well and acrimonious disputes seem to have been quite common, some ending in bloodshed.

So when the harbour was being extended by diverting the river Frome, Henry III sent a letter addressed to 'all his honest men dwelling in Redcliff''. He wrote of how the burgesses of Bristol, 'for the common benefit of the town and your suburb', had begun this work on digging what was called 'the great trench' and commanded the Redcliff men to lend them assistance so the work would receive no delay.

Redcliff became incorporated into Bristol but its parish church of St Mary was considered finer than any other Bristol one. Queen Elizabeth I is quoted as going so far as to say it was the goodliest, fairest parish church in all England. It was not always in as impressive a shape as when she saw it. The first church, dating to Norman times, fell into decay and was completely rebuilt, suffered neglect and was then restored again.

The church had great benefactors in the Canynges family, wealthy merchants. William Canynges the Elder was responsible in 1376 for a rebuilding in the Perpendicular style. Some sort of disaster must have happened to this church because in 1442 his grandson William Canynges the Younger, who was mayor of Bristol, 'kept masons and workmen to repair and edifye, cover and glaze the church of Redcliffe'.

William Canynges the Younger had extensive business interests, trading overseas with Prussia, Iceland and Finland. After his wife died, he gave up his wealth and took holy orders. In the church there is a richly decorated Canynges tomb where his wife, Joan, is buried, containing both their effigies underneath the ornate canopy, but nearby a simpler alabaster figure shows him in his priest's robes. His legacy was indeed a magnificent building, but for centuries the spire, which was struck by lightning in 1445 and partially collapsed, remained in a truncated condition.

It was in the 1840s, with evidence that the fabric of the church was deteriorating, that it became obvious that something would have to be done. A survey was carried

*Above*: William Canynges the Younger's tomb effigy.

*Right*: St Mary Redcliffe spire towering above the trees.

Eighteenth-century Redcliffe Parade viewed from Redcliffe Bridge.

out, reporting that it was vital that a 'solid substantial repair' be carried out 'to reinstate it to its ancient and pristine beauty'. As part of the lengthy process, hovels that had been built up against the walls were swept away, decayed stonework from buttresses to tracery was replaced and eventually the soaring spire restored to its proper height. On 9 May 1872 the capstone of the spire was laid by the mayor, whose wife also travelled up to the top with him, firstly in a wooden cage powered by a steam engine, then for the last 50 feet by a primitive plank lift powered by workmen with ropes.

Nowadays the name of the church is usually written as St Mary Redcliffe, yet where it stands is Redcliff Hill. Nineteenth-century newspapers were not consistent, spelling it sometimes with and sometimes without the final 'e' at various times, so there seems to be no definite year to mark the change.

# Royal West of England Academy

Back in 1844 a group of artists and patrons met together to discuss the founding of a Bristol Academy for the Promotion of the Fine Arts. While some citizens subscribed £25 towards the project and others were even more generous with donations of £100, by far the largest amount of money given was by Mrs Sharples – a magnificent £2,000.

Ellen Sharples had been a talented pupil of Bristol artist James Sharples, whom she subsequently married and travelled with to America where they lived for a while. They had three children, Felix, James Junior and Rolinda, all of whom also became artists, although Rolinda is the best known with her pictorial representations of real life. When her husband died in 1811, Ellen and her daughter returned to Bristol and both of them exhibited work at the Royal Academy in London.

Rolinda died in 1838 and James Junior a year later. When the Bristol Academy was proposed, Ellen decided that she would give financial support to this new institution. So she contributed her £2,000 and when she died in 1849 she left a bequest amounting to a further £4,000. Although the Academy operated in premises at St Augustine's Back for some years, land was acquired in Queen's Road where a brand-new building was erected, completed in 1857.

Originally there was a forecourt with steps at the entrance, but in 1912 a new front 'of a strictly Classical character' was added, also creating a spacious lobby. Renamed the Royal West of England Academy by order of King George V, the royal arms are prominently carved in stone over the central doorway. The two large statues in niches, of Flaxman and Reynolds, date from the 1857 building.

The RWA presents a varied exhibition programme, including, as from the beginning, the annual Open Exhibitions.

Royal West of England Academy in Queens Road.

# Stokes Croft

Stokes Croft has had a chequered history. It was known as Berewyke's Croft originally, no doubt belonging to a member of the family of that name who lived in Bristol in the thirteenth century. A hundred years on the owner of the property was John Stoke, mayor in 1364, 1366 and 1379, and although he died in 1382, his surname has stuck right down to the present day.

The footpath that ran through this piece of land developed into a road leading north to Gloucester. Outside the city walls, this was an important guarded route during the Civil War and there were fierce fights between Royalists and Parliamentarians due to its proximity to Prior's Hill Fort just up Nine Tree Hill. In the first half of the eighteenth century the scene here was more peaceful, though the Stokes Croft Theatre at the foot of Nine Tree Hill offered excitement with a variety of entertainments, plays, pantomime and acrobatic acts.

There was a turnpike gate at the end of Stokes Croft and Roque's 1741 map of Bristol shows a few buildings on either side of the road which led to it. One of these was the Baptist College, which started in 1720, although there had been money left by Edward Terrill many years before in the hope of such a foundation.

Stokes Croft Vintage Market – from retro furniture to vintage clothes.

Later came the Dissenting Charity Almshouses and School. The school, built in 1772 next to the existing almshouse, was endowed by a group of businessmen, mainly from the Lewins Mead Meeting. To begin with twenty boys were taught there, although the number doubled later.

By 1775 buildings that had been private houses with large gardens were used by an increasing number of the residents for business purposes. A century later shopfronts had been inserted in most of the older houses and some specially designed new premises had been built, such as the Perry & Co. Carriageworks. Built in 1862, pennant and Bath stone arcading fronted this famous example of Bristol Byzantine work by architect Edward William Godwin.

Stokes Croft became a busy shopping area but things began to change again. There had been bomb damage during the war, of course, causing the loss of the school, amongst other buildings. The Carriageworks had a prominent and unsuitably tall office block called Westmorland House thrust alongside it. Gradually, from the 1970s, shops that had been there for many years closed and several dance clubs opened up. The area, having become home to small businesses and artists, began to be labelled as 'bohemian' and 'alternative' with a 'vibrant and liberal attitude'.

Now two of the clubs are probably closing, with premises set to be given alternative uses as accommodation. The Carriageworks, which has suffered blight and deterioration for such a long time, is now having its frontage incorporated into a

No. 51 Stokes Croft.

Carriage Works in Stokes Croft before development.

development of housing and business units and Westmorland House has been demolished. Are things about to change radically again?

# Suspension Bridge

The bridge across the Avon Gorge might well have looked so different. When Alderman Vick left his money towards bridging the 750-foot gap midway through the eighteenth century he was no doubt imagining something far more conventional, certainly of stone. The money was left to accrue interest and after forty years a design was duly presented. It would have filled the gorge with two apartment blocks connected by a giant arch through which ships could navigate the river and above which crossings would be made, all topped with a series of spires. It never got past the design stage.

In 1827 rumours began circulating about the amount of money now available due to the interest on the original sum and a local newspaper commented that the provision of a suspension bridge, 'a recent discovery of a more enlightened age', rather than a stone one could be more practical and no doubt more economical. Two years later a recently formed committee bought land on the Leigh Woods side of the river from Sir John Smyth of Ashton Court, then called for designs of a suspension bridge to be submitted.

Isambard Kingdom Brunel was then twenty-four years old and had been an engineer practically from birth, it seems, inheriting and expanding on his father's skills. Prolific in ideas, he entered four designs out of the twenty put before the committee. Thomas Telford, who had become famous for his Menai and Conwy suspension bridges, was brought in to adjudicate and being a man of rather rigid ideas, argued that the width of the gorge was too great for a single span from one side to the other. He prepared a design of his own where massive piers would rise from the sides of the river below, thus supporting a three-span bridge.

Although the committee may have approved it, public opinion did not. There were accusations that such a bridge would dominate and obscure the landscape, not float above it and demands were made for a rethink. Telford's idea was pushed aside and

*Close-up of Clifton Suspension Bridge viewed from Sion Hill.*

one of Brunel's designs was chosen. It may have been a triumphant day for him, but there was a hard road ahead and he was never to see the bridge completed.

Financial problems, partly caused by the Bristol Riots of 1831, meant that the actual foundation stone ceremony was not held until 1836 and work progressed slowly even after that. There were two piers and not much else, as money had run out, when in 1844 a newspaper article complained, 'We commence a suspension bridge, sink thousands in the erection of a couple of unsightly piers which stand as monuments to our folly and leave the bridge unsuspended.'

There were frequent proposals that the seemingly useless piers should be demolished and when Brunel died in September 1859, his obituary made reference to these 'mortifying monuments of utter failure'. A new company was formed the next year to restart work, assisted by the fact that the chains became available from the Brunel-designed Hungerford Bridge, London, which was being replaced. This time progress on the project was more speedy and successful and the bridge was opened on 7 December 1864, with great pomp and ceremony.

Suspension Bridge viewed from the entrance to Brunel Lock.

# Temple

The real name of Temple parish church is Holy Cross. That was the dedication of the oval church built by a group of Knights Templar on this land, south of the River Avon, that they had been given in 1145. The knights had authority to export wool and cloth and Temple parish became home to many weavers. The Company of Weavers were granted the right of a chapel in the church in 1299, dedicated to St Catherine.

The foundations of the first church lie buried beneath later rebuilding. The Knights Templar order fell into disrepute, which may or may not have been completely deserved. Increasingly rich and powerful, they attracted many enemies and were abolished in 1312. Everything they owned became the property of the Knights Hospitaller but the name of the Templars still lingers on.

Temple church was rebuilt in the fourteenth century in the traditional English style. It became famous because of its tower. According to an old poem, 'This Temple

Temple Church tower from Victoria Street.

tower, like Pisa's own, Doth lean and bend and seem to fall.' The top of the 114-foot tower is nearly 5 foot 5 inches out of true. Not only that, it kinks in the middle. It has been that way for centuries.

The westward lean of the tower developed within a short time of its construction, the foundations not adequate for the marshy ground on which it was built. The upper stage was built to counteract this and was completed in 1460, according to William Worcestre, 'for ringing and sounding the splendid bells'. In fact, when the Duke of Norfolk visited around 100 years later, he was shown how ringing those bells could pulverise a small stone placed in the chink between the leaning tower and the church.

The bells ring no more here though; they are in Bristol Cathedral. The church was a casualty of the Blitz and very little could be saved, not enough to even start to restore it. So only the skeletal ruins remain to give an indication of how it must have looked in its glory days with its long chancel lit by tall windows.

Temple Meads were the meadows once owned by the Knights Templar, outside the city wall, which was entered by Temple Gate. On Temple Meads was erected the terminus of the Great Western Railway, built to connect Bristol with London. Isambard Kingdom Brunel was appointed Chief Engineer and his station building still fronts the road with its castle-like appearance. The first section of the track, to Bath, was travelled by around 6,000 of the excited public on 31 August 1840 and a year later they could make the whole journey to London in four hours. Nowadays there are newer station buildings, far more destinations and faster trains.

Temple Quay regeneration scheme was begun at the end of the twentieth century on land once covered by the goods yard of the station. This was an area of dereliction, buildings having been demolished, and it was decided that it should be developed, offering a chance for a new commercial centre close to the station for transport advantages, expanding to housing.

*Below left*: Glazed roof of Brunel's train shed at Temple Meads.

*Below right*: Statue of Brunel at Temple Quay.

# Thekla

The *Thekla* was built in Germany in 1958 and spent most of the first part of her life as a coastal freight steamer, carrying cargoes of timber. She ran aground in 1976 and after salvage, was left to rust. Bought by Vivian Stanshall and his wife, Ki Longfellow-Stanshall, the *Thekla* was renamed the *Old Profanity Showboat* and brought to Bristol to be a floating theatre. As well as theatrical productions, the boat became a popular performance space for jazz and folk bands and comedians.

Later, taken over by new owners, the *Thekla* was refurbished in 2006, remaining a music venue with a capacity of around 350. It may not be to everyone's tastes but there is no doubt that thousands of people have enjoyed hearing the live music that is so much a part of this unusual setting.

The *Thekla* at The Grove.

# Mr Thompson of the Seven Stars

Back in the 1780s the Seven Stars in Thomas Lane was very much a sailors' pub, not just serving them with drinks but providing them with bed and board between their voyages. William Thompson, the landlord, got on well with his customers and listened to the tales of their times at sea, some of which filled him with horror. From them he learned much about the slave ships, from the squalid conditions below decks to the inhumane treatment that was carried out, and also how some sailors had been tricked into becoming crew members.

When Thomas Clarkson started on his long and arduous campaign towards the abolition of slavery by visiting British ports to gain information, he was introduced to Thompson in Bristol. Finding out facts at first hand was a risky business but Thompson, a sympathiser to the cause, was of invaluable help, knowing where sailors of the slave ships could be found without asking questions that would raise suspicions. This provided Clarkson with more vital information to report to the *Society for Effecting the Abolition of the Slave Trade*, which he had helped to found.

It took twenty more years after Clarkson's visit to William Thompson at the Seven Stars before the Abolition of the Slave Trade Act was passed by Parliament, but

The Seven Stars in Thomas Lane.

opposition to the trade had been building steadily during that time from all levels of society. The number of Bristol ships involved in the trade had dwindled significantly, reflecting the increasing distaste that was shown. William Thompson can be proudly remembered as one of those who played a part in bringing this to an end.

# Thunderbolt Square

Thunderbolt Street was said to be the shortest street in Bristol. Now it no longer exists at all. It ran from King Street to Alderskey Lane by Broad Quay but in 1900 a block of land was acquired by the Cooperative Wholesale Society for warehousing. During excavation work for this, cannonballs were found and presented to the museum. The CWS building dominated the Quayhead until demolition in 1973 and replacement by Broad Quay House.

When alterations were made at the end of King Street adjoining Queen Square and a roundabout was removed, it enabled a small public square to be incorporated. This was named Thunderbolt Square to commemorate the vanished street.

Thunderbolt Square near King Street.

# Unicorns

It may come as a surprise to suddenly notice the pair of 12-foot-tall golden unicorns that prance on the end blocks of the roof of the sober-looking City Hall (formerly known as the Council House). Indeed, it was a surprise to the council members, let alone the citizens of Bristol, when the two turned up in 1950. After all, the foundation stone had been laid in 1938 – it had taken all those years to build because of the Second World War, and no one had previously mentioned unicorns. After the return of the architect E. Vincent Harris from his holiday, he confirmed that they were meant to be up on the roof, so up they went.

Unicorns are supporters on the arms of the City and County of Bristol. The arms themselves date from the fourteenth century, and the supporters and crest were added by a grant dated 24 August 1569. In heraldry, the unicorn is considered a sign of virtue, allied to courage and strength. The motto reflects that – 'Virtute et Industria', 'by virtue and industry' – but it was added later than the grant of 1569.

*Above left*: One of a pair of unicorns by David McFall on City Hall (Council House).

*Above right*: Until 1961 Bristol buses displayed the city's coat of arms with its unicorn supporters.

# University

In the 1870s there was concern that Bristol was lagging behind other cities in providing education beyond school-leaving age. This had been forcibly expressed by John Percival, headmaster of Clifton College, writing to Oxford University colleges giving his views. Following his lead, other prominent citizens voiced their agreement. This led to the foundation of University College, an institution supplying for both sexes 'a means of continuing their studies in science, especially applied sciences, languages, history and literature'.

This opened its doors in 1876, using temporary premises at first before permanent buildings were erected in Queens Road, which were designed by C. W. Hansom. The college depended heavily on subscriptions and bequests made by benefactors from Bristol as well as the students' fees to keep things going. The Bristol Medical School was incorporated with the college in the 1890s and with the beginning of a new century there was increasing action towards gaining a charter for full university status.

It took until 1909 before that result was achieved. The promise of a donation of £100,000 from the Wills family had prompted a snowball effect, as it encouraged many others to pledge their support. The charter was approved by King Edward VII and the university became a reality.

*Below left*: Wills Memorial Tower at the top of Park Street.

*Below right*: Royal Fort House in Tyndalls Park.

Dominating the top of Park Street, the 215-foot Wills Memorial Tower, completed in 1925, is perhaps looked on as the symbolic heart of the university and graduation ceremonies are held in its Great Hall. The university is made up of many schools and departments divided into six faculties, occupying a fascinating variety of buildings, some old, some much more modern.

The Victoria Rooms, rising like a Roman temple behind bronze sea creature-themed fountains, is used by the Department of Music. It dates from 1842, designed as an assembly rooms by Charles Dyer, the columned front topped by a pediment representing Wisdom in a chariot ushering in Morning. It was a popular venue for not only concerts but horticultural shows, dramatic readings, civic balls and association dinners for over seventy-five years. It was acquired by the university in 1920 and served as the headquarters of the Students' Union for some years. Now it has been returned to a musical use once more.

Royal Fort House took its name from the fortifications that previously existed on the site during the Civil War. The house was built in the mid-eighteenth century for Thomas Tyndall and contains beautiful plasterwork featuring pastoral motifs. It is set on a rise, in gardens landscaped by Humphrey Repton that were once part of what was called Mr Tyndall's Park.

In contrast, the School of Chemistry building was originally a 1960s five-storey block, refurbished with state-of-the-art laboratories and reopened in 1999, while ten years later the Centre for Nanoscience and Quantum Information came into being and is known as the quietest building in the world. Now an additional campus focusing on digital technologies and innovation is in the process of being erected on the site of the former Royal Mail sorting office by Temple Meads.

The Victoria Rooms in Queens Road.

# V

## Vachell, Ada

Though born into a well-to-do Cardiff family in 1866, Ada had her share of suffering yet was no shirker when it came to hard work for charitable causes. In 1874 her brother and sister died of scarlet fever, to which she also fell victim, surviving with partial deafness in both ears. A few months later her parents brought her and her young brother to live in Clifton.

Charitable work was important to Ada. She volunteered at the Children's Help Society camps at Langford and Winscombe, for children from the poorest parts of Bristol. These were organised to give 250 boys and 150 girls each year the chance to have a week's holiday in the country. Later she helped run a club for factory girls. It was with the disabled that she made her mark, though. Inspired by the Guild of Poor Brave Things that had been set up in London, she founded a similar organisation in Bristol. This not only provided disadvantaged and disabled children with a fortnight's holiday in the country, but also catered for adults, offering social activities including lectures and helping young people find apprenticeships.

A tireless fundraiser, Ada expanded the guild, opening purpose-built premises in 1913 in Braggs Lane, St Jude's, where crafts could be taught too, the name changing four years after to Guild of the Handicapped. Involved in other projects as well, she still found time to campaign for votes for women.

All this constant work must have been a drain on her strength. She contracted pneumonia and died in December 1923.

Blue plaque to Ada Vachell at Foley Cottage, Clyde Road.

## Wallace and Gromit

Created by Bristol-based Aardman Animations, Wallace and Gromit first appeared in the 1990 short film *A Grand Day Out*. In their films Wallace, a cheese-loving inventor from Wigan, and his more than intelligent dog Gromit experience an amazing and often hair-raising range of adventures, thwarting villains though leaving destruction in their wake. Using stop motion technique, shot one frame at a time after moving the clay models, the filming is a slow process and requires great precision.

The Wallace and Gromit Grand Appeal is the Bristol Children's Hospital Charity. It supports projects from pioneering medical equipment to arts and play activities to respite care. One of its fundraising activities, in 2013, was the Gromit Unleashed Trail when eighty giant Gromit sculptures, painted by a mix of local and celebrity artists, were placed around the streets of Bristol for ten weeks during summer and attracted over 1.1 million people. At the end each sculpture was auctioned and the money donated to the appeal. In 2018 this was followed up with a Gromit Unleashed 2 Trail, also featuring Wallace and Feathers McGraw sculptures. So far, since 1995, the Grand Appeal has raised £50 million to support sick babies and children and their families in Bristol Children's Hospital.

Private Gromit sculpture on display outside the Bristol Royal Hospital for Children.

# Wapping Wharf

Wapping Wharf has blossomed since 2006, when Bristol City Council approved a plan to bring this area back to life by creating a range of new homes, local shops and services. Just across the Cut from Southville and linked by Gaol Ferry Bridge, this would also provide a pedestrian and cycle way into the heart of Bristol via Gaol Ferry Steps.

As the names of the bridge and steps imply, on Cumberland Road once stood the massive gaol that was completed in 1820, a solid block of a building. *Mathews' Bristol Guide* of the time was enthusiastic, describing it as 'extensive and commodious' and 'commanding extensive views of the countryside'. The building was engulfed by fire during the 1831 riots and had to be rebuilt. It was closed in 1883 due to significant deterioration, a new prison having been constructed at Horfield.

The site was sold to the GWR for use as a coal yard, so most of the buildings and walls were demolished; only the entrance wall and gatehouse remain. Over the years the gatehouse decayed more and more to resemble a ruined castle but now, as part of the Wapping Wharf development, it has been stabilised. It will be renovated and front a pedestrian path through the homes being built.

CARGO is a retail area made of converted shipping containers on two levels, featuring a variety of restaurants and shops. With many having glass frontages, they make a striking addition to this once derelict part of the harbour.

Wapping Wharf from Gaol Ferry Steps.

The Gaol Gatehouse on Cumberland Road.

Wapping Wharf restaurants and shops.

# Wesley, John

John Wesley spent many hours on horseback travelling from place to place, preaching in the open air. It was something he wouldn't ever have contemplated in his early career as a clergyman. After seeing his evangelical friend George Whitefield preaching to a group, he understood how he also could reach those who would never set foot inside a church, those who were ignored and looked down on by so many ministers.

Wesley made his first open-air sermon in Avon Street, St Philips, Bristol in April 1739 and during his life journeyed hundreds of thousands of miles addressing crowds all over the country. Of course, if he was welcomed into a church in order to preach, he would accept, but these occasions were few, as he was seen as challenging the ideology and hierarchical authority of the Established Church. He was, it was said, threatening the very order of the country with his opinions and interpretation of the Bible's teachings, known as Methodism.

The New Room in Bristol was built as a meeting place for those who had heard him and Whitefield and wanted further instruction. Wesley cared about the poor; he knew others did not, seeing it to be 'in the natural order of things'. So he provided not only comfort and encouragement but medicines, clothing and money to those who were in need. He believed strongly in education, that each individual is valuable and should continue in lifelong learning. He equipped lay preachers to go out and spread the Methodist ideas all over the country. The Preachers' Rooms, where they stayed between journeys, are still in place above the New Room Chapel.

John's brother Charles, also a clergyman, went on evangelical journeys for twenty years and preached many sermons, both then and afterwards, but is probably best known for writing around 6,000 hymns, including the carol 'Hark the Herald Angels Sing'. The house where he lived in Charles Street, Bristol also still stands.

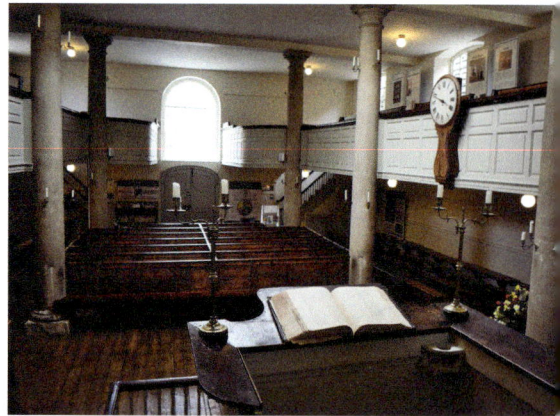

*Above*: Inside the New Room.

*Left*: Statue of John Wesley on horseback by A. G. Walker in New Room courtyard.

# X

## Xenon

Xenon is a dense, colourless and odourless gas. So what does it have to do with Bristol? The city has long been known as a centre of scientific study and medical research. Research by Marianne Thoresen, Professor of Neonatal Neuroscience at the University of Bristol, showed that cooling new-born babies who had been starved of oxygen during birth could reduce their risk of suffering brain damage. With Dr John Dingley of Swansea University's College of Medicine, a technique was developed for cooling the babies by delivering xenon through a closed-circuit system in a neonatal ventilator.

Dowry Square, home of the Pneumatic Institute.

First used in 2010 at St Michael's Hospital, Bristol where Professor Thoreson was Consultant Neonatologist, this treatment using xenon doubles the protective effect of cooling on the brain. Since then it has been carried out all across the UK, saving hundreds of babies born at full term but at risk of dying or suffering brain injury caused by a lack of oxygen or blood supply at birth.

In 1793 physician and scientist Thomas Beddoes set out to investigate the medical powers of gases in a basement laboratory in Hotwells. He was eager to find a cure for tuberculosis, as many of his patients had tried the local Hotwell waters without success. Five years later, having moved to Dowry Square, he founded the Pneumatic Institute, using equipment designed by James Watt and taking on as superintendent a young Cornishman named Humphry Davy.

Conducting experiments with nitrous oxide, Davy used himself as a guinea pig, both in the institute and outside, using a silk air bag. On at least one occasion he shocked a passing stranger by in turn fainting and laughing uncontrollably. His friends the poets Samuel Taylor Coleridge and Robert Southey also participated, with Southey penning lyrical letters to his brothers about his experiences. Davy wrote up a report on his research and the effects of the gas with case studies, running to 580 pages.

Davy was well aware of the anaesthetic effects of nitrous oxide, but it was quite a while before it began to be used in dentistry. Anyway, the publication of his report made his reputation and he was off to London. In 1800 he took up an appointment as assistant lecturer in chemistry at the Royal Institution, going on to become a fellow of the Royal Society. Being alerted to the danger of methane gas to miners, who used helmet candles for light, he invented a safety lamp, which was known as the Davy lamp.

Davy became Sir Humphry in 1818. By then Thomas Beddoes had been dead for a decade. The scientific aspects of the Pneumatic Institute did not survive for long and it must be considered as having failed in its aspirations, becoming a hospital for the poor for Beddoes' last few remaining years. He was buried in the Strangers' Burial Ground in Clifton, so named because it was so often the resting place for those visitors to Bristol who had died while taking the waters at the Hotwell in hope of a cure.

# Y

## Yeamans, Robert

Robert Yeamans should have been a contented man. He was a successful merchant, occupying a fine house in Wine Street with his expanding family and had recently held the position of Sheriff of Bristol. Despite all this, he felt little satisfaction. It was 1643, the Civil War had torn the country in two. Now the Parliamentarians held Bristol

St John's Arch once had a fortified gate where the conspirators intended to overpower the guards.

and Yeamans was a Royalist. Hearing that the king's troops under Prince Rupert were heading towards the city, he and others, including fellow merchant George Boucher, plotted to admit them so they could overpower the occupying forces.

The city was still walled with guarded gates. The route of entry, it was decided, would be by St John's Gate where the guard would be surprised by a group of armed Royalist sympathisers who were going to wear white ribbons so they could be identified. The gate would then be opened and the city taken. At least that was the plan, but someone talked and the plot was discovered on 9 March before it could be carried out.

Just after midnight it was reported to the Parliamentary commanders in Bristol that a group of men had gathered together in Yeamans' house while others were in Boucher's in Christmas Street. An officer and forty musketeers were despatched to Wine Street, where they were met with some resistance but realising that the game was up, Yeamans and twenty-four men surrendered and were taken prisoner. The group in Boucher's house were also overcome and all the plotters were taken under guard to the castle.

Yeamans and Boucher were kept in chains in the castle dungeon for three months and were then sentenced to death. The decision was to hang Yeamans on gallows outside his own front door but the old Corn Market stood in the way 'perched upon pillars like a rickety wheat stack', so the gallows was set up at Guard House Passage nearby and that was where he met his end on 30 May.

Although the Royalist army did not get into the city by trickery, in July some of Prince Rupert's forces managed to breach the defences between two of the forts. The Parliamentarians surrendered and were allowed to march away. Rupert was appointed General of the entire Royalist army but things did not go so well for him subsequently. In the summer of 1645, after a defeat, he retreated to Bristol and was besieged. Humiliated, he had to surrender Bristol to the Parliamentarians once more.

# Z

## Zed Alley

This alley was used as a route from the old Stone Bridge at the head of the Quay, crossing Host Street then climbing to Steep Street, which was a main road out of the city. The lower section from the quayside zig-zagged, as clearly shown on Roque's map of 1741 – hence the name – but that was straightened in the 1920s to provide 'an easy gradient path' and so took away the distinctive shape.

When the city was inspected in the middle of the nineteenth century for the Board of Health, Zed Alley was described as branching out of Host Street as a long narrow passage with a privy at the top where it joined Steep Street. Even when coaches had used Steep Street on their way to Gloucester and the ferry to Wales, it had been a tight squeeze, and included a sharp bend, so it was radically altered in the 1870s. Not only was the roadway widened and old houses removed, it was renamed Colston Street as by then the Colston Hall, a new public hall, had been erected at the bottom on the site

Zed Alley from Host Street.

of the school, founded by the merchant, which had moved to Stapleton. The name of the Colston Hall itself is now set to change in the near future.

There's nothing glamorous about Zed Alley; it's just a functional path that has been used by thousands of people over the centuries, an ancient right of way of which so many have been erased or built over. It is a piece of Bristol history that still remains in place.

# Zoo

The Bristol and Clifton Zoological Gardens, to give it the correct name, came into being in 1835 when 12 acres of land was purchased by a company of 220 shareholders, a group which consisted of many of the prominent citizens of Bristol, who thought it worthwhile to stump up the £25 per share required. They engaged a London landscape gardener, Richard Forrest, to lay out the site, which featured winding paths round and radiating out from a central irregular-shaped lake covering 2 acres, leading to enclaves containing various animal houses bordered by 'select and rare specimens' of trees. An old limekiln became the basis for a bear pit and there were several monkey poles flanking the avenue from the entrance as well as smaller pools for fish and aquatic birds.

Fundraising was apparently key from the start. In 1838 a fete, complete with fireworks, was held so the proceeds could be used to purchase a pair of lions. In fact, it proved quite a popular venue for fetes among groups as varied as the Total Abstinence Society to the Independent Order of Oddfellows. The number of animals increased as well, by natural means like a llama giving birth or acquisitions such as a Bengal tiger and an emu.

Elephants were always favourites among the animals. There was one called Zebi, who lived at the zoo for around forty years from 1868, followed by Rajah in the early twentieth century, Rosie in the 1940s and '50s and Wendy who died in 2002. In his day the most well-known zoo inhabitant was Alfred the gorilla who grew to be extremely large on his vegetarian diet.

Towards the end of the twentieth century changes started to be made, to take the zoo forward into a more modern form. These changes included a new aquarium and the reptile house and monkey house. The conservation aspect is extremely important to the zoo, stressing the value of nature to young and old by developing exhibits, as well as participating in projects to protect endangered animals all over the world.

The meerkats have long been favourites at Bristol Zoo. (Misty Morning Photography)